# Real Estate Tax Strategy

Use a Self-Directed IRA or
Other Retirement Plan to
Purchase Real Estate

Joseph Starzyk

ISBN: 1523352000
ISBN-13: 978-1523352005

# Table of Contents

# Chapter 1:
## What is an IRA?

An IRA is an Individual Retirement Account. Primarily, its purpose is to provide funds for your retirement for whatever your needs may be. The government considers you retired once you reach the age of 59 ½. Once you have attained that age, even if you are still working, you have full access to the funds available in your account.

As we will see later, there are several types of IRA accounts available. The one most people think of when they think of an IRA is called a Traditional IRA. Generally, you get a tax deduction when you contribute money to a Traditional IRA. The money grows tax-free until you decide, or are forced, to make a withdrawal from your account. Though tax-free is the term often used, tax deferred is a more accurate term. You pay tax on the earnings; however, it is delayed until you make a withdrawal. When you take a distribution from the account years later, you are generally taxed on the full amount. The tax rate is based on your taxable income for that year.

The growth of funds in an IRA is traditionally characterized by stocks, bonds, etc. A stockbroker would handle the portfolio (or collection) of funds in your account. They would invest in a variety of stocks, bonds, index funds, mutual funds, and other items depending on your risk tolerance, age, and other criteria. More recently, individuals have started to manage their own portfolios.

Since the earnings in the account are tax deferred, growth is compounded. Year after year, instead of paying a percentage of your earnings to the government, the funds get reinvested. The power of compounded earnings is incredible. This is considered one of the main benefits of an IRA and other retirement plans.

Withdrawing funds prior to full retirement age has a significant tax impact. Not only are you taxed on the full distribution, but you are often subject to a 10% penalty on the amount withdrawn. You may also be subject to additional state tax penalties. It is difficult to re-fund your IRA once funds have been withdrawn.

The IRA is a popular saving option for those who are employed, but whose employer does not offer a retirement plan. It is also used frequently by self-employed individuals to help save for retirement. The IRA has changed little over the years. Its rules are well-known. You have plenty of options to choose from when opening an account. Keep in mind, the

IRA is just one type of tool that you can use to take charge of your retirement plans.

# Chapter 2:
# Definition of a Self-Directed IRA or Retirement Plan

You may be thinking: "well, if I get to choose the investments in my IRA, aren't I already self-directing?" Well, yes and no. This is really just a play on words. Self-directed is the term used to describe what kind of investments the plan can purchase. A self-directed IRA (SDIRA) can invest in substantially more types of investments than a regular IRA. This is the one major difference that sets apart the SDIRA.

As we will see in the next section, several types of plans can be considered self-directed. A self-directed plan can purchase the following types of investments:
- Stocks, bonds, mutual funds, CDs, etc.
- Rental properties
- Land
- Debt instruments/notes
- Private stock
- Private companies, such as LLCs
- Tax liens
- Precious metals, such as gold, silver, etc.
- Most anything held for investment purposes

The rules are written to describe what a self-directed plan cannot invest in. The list is rather short, and it includes:

- Collectibles, such as artwork, certain metals, gems, most coins, antiques, stamps, alcohol, rugs, etc.

- Life insurance contracts/policies

You also cannot enter into transactions with certain related people. We will touch on this and the items above again later in the book. As you may have guessed from the title, this book will assume you are using or are going to use a self-directed plan to invest in real estate.

# Chapter 3:
# Eligible Self-Directed Retirement Plans

Though often referred to as a SDIRA, many different retirement plans can be self-directed. Examples include the following:
- Traditional IRA
- Roth IRA
- Simplified Employee Pension (SEP) plan
- Savings Incentive Match Plan (SIMPLE)
- Spousal IRA
- Employer 401(k) plan
- Section 457 plan
- Section 403(b) plan
- Defined Benefit plan
- Solo 401(k) plan
- Coverdell Education Savings Account
- Health Savings Account (HSA)

We will go into more detail on the three most popular groups for our purposes. This includes the Traditional and Roth IRAs, the SEP and SIMPLE plans, and the Solo 401(k) plan. Each option has its pros and cons. Remember, all of these plans can be set up as a self-directed plan in order to invest in real estate.

### Traditional and Roth IRAs

The fundamental difference between a Traditional and Roth IRA is when the money gets taxed. Contributions to a Traditional IRA are generally deductible in the year made. When distributions are taken from the account, the full amount of the distribution is taxable. On the flip side, contributions to a Roth IRA are not deductible at all. However, when you take a distribution from a Roth IRA, none of it is taxable.

Following are the pros and cons of both types of plans (applies to both types unless specified):

**Pros:**
- Easy to set up
- Reasonable fees
- Available to employees and the self-employed
- Earnings accumulate tax-deferred
- Current year tax benefit for the Traditional IRA
- No reporting required to IRS
- Access to original contributions to Roth IRA

**Cons:**
- Uncertain tax rates: future tax rates may be higher than current rates (primarily impacts Traditional IRAs – opposite for Roth IRAs)
- There are income limits to contribute to a Roth IRA (ignoring back-door contributions)
- Annual contribution limits are low

- There are income limits to the amount of deductible contributions to a Traditional IRA depending on how you/your spouse are covered
- Funds for traditional IRA are tied up until retirement age, with minimum exceptions to take a distribution prior to reaching retirement age
- No loan option
- Required minimum distributions begin at the age of 70 ½ for a Traditional IRA

## SEP and SIMPLE Plans

These plans were established for self-employed individuals to save more of their earnings into retirement accounts. Prior to the changes made to the Solo 401(k) plan, they also provided individuals with the opportunity to set aside the highest dollar amount of cash. Though a SEP plan and 401(k) plan have the same maximum contributions, ignoring catch-up contributions, a participant is able to reach the maximum level with less earnings for a 401(k) plan.

If you have no employees, the only real difference between the two is the annual contribution limits. A SEP plan would provide higher maximum limits than a SIMPLE plan.

For those with employees, the primary difference is the funding options (along with the contribution limits) for the two. In a SEP plan, all contributions are made by the employer. They must be proportional across the board for all employees. The owner also gets an additional contribution that is based on the net profit of the business for the year. In a SIMPLE plan, both the employees (including yourself) and employer are eligible to make contributions. Again, the employer can make an additional contribution based on their net earnings from self-employment.

Following are the pros and cons of both types of plans:

### Pros:
- Easy to set up
- Reasonable fees
- Earnings accumulate tax-deferred
- Can deduct current year contributions
- No reporting required to IRS
- Can be used even if you have employees

### Cons:
- No Roth option
- Only available to the self-employed
- No loan option
- Annual contributions limits are higher than Traditional or Roth plans, but still lower than a 401(k) plan
- Required minimum distributions must begin at the age of 70 ½

For further reading, including annual contribution limits, be sure to check out the IRS' Publication 560.

### Solo 401(k) Plan

This plan is also known as an Individual 401(k), Solo-K, Uni-K, or Self-Employed 401(k). Including catch-up contributions, this plan allows for the highest contribution limits among the self-employed. It operates similar to a traditional employee/employer 401(k) plan. However, the self-employed individual can make contributions as both the employee and employer.

Unique to 401(k) plans is the ability to take out loans on the account. You generally can borrow 50% of your account value, up to $50,000, tax-free. You can use these funds for whatever purpose you want. There is a usually a small processing fee, and you have to include interest when repaying the loan. This is not necessarily a bad thing since you are contributing the interest directly to your retirement account anyways. If you are using the loan for a business purpose, your business could deduct the interest expense as well.

You can also designate a Roth account within your 401(k) plan. You are able to contribute to the Roth (after-tax) portion of your account, or the traditional pre-tax portion.

Following are the pros and cons of the Solo 401(k) plan:

**Pros:**

- Highest contribution limit among all retirement plans for the self-employed
- Loan option for penalty-free access to funds prior to retirement age
- Earnings accumulate tax-deferred
- Roth option is available
- Can deduct current year contributions for pre-tax option

- Possible protection against creditors
- Not charged unrelated debt financed income taxes (we will cover this later)

**Cons:**

- More administrative requirements due to IRS reporting requirements
- Fees are generally higher than other types of plans
- Required minimum distributions must begin at the age of 70 ½ for non-Roth portion

Options abound for self-directed retirement plans. If you are looking for flexibility and high contribution limits, you may find the Solo 401(k) plan will work best for you. Your advisor should be able to help you choose a plan type that is right for you.

# Chapter 4:
# You vs. Your IRA vs. Your Plan Administrator vs. Your Custodian

**K**nowing who is in charge of what will help you understand your retirement plan. Ultimately, when dealing with these self-directed plans, it is your account and your responsibility to manage them.

A custodian, sometimes known as the trustee or a trust company, must be a bank, a federally insured credit union, a savings and loan association, or an entity approved by the IRS. A custodian would handle the formation and ongoing paperwork required for your retirement account. They are also in charge of your account's funds, can hold title to assets and other investments, and can issue payments such as checks. Custodians are highly regulated and must continue to meet strict requirements. A custodian is required for all IRA types. You will receive a letter from the custodian stating that the plan you have chosen is operating according to the rules that the IRS has put in place.

A plan administrator appears to be similar to a custodian, but, in actuality, their role and responsibilities vary considerably. Like a custodian, a plan administrator can handle the formation and ongoing paperwork required for your retirement account. They also assist in the account's maintenance. However, a plan administrator would use a custodian for your account. Basically, the plan administrator acts as the middle man between your account and your custodian. Some plan administrators can accept contributions and process distributions as well. They would settle these funds with the custodian. Plan administrators do not have any federal oversight and are not regulated by the IRS.

Again, as mentioned at the start of the chapter, the account holder is primarily responsible and can often be held legally liable for their retirement account. It is important to remember that you are in charge of these accounts. While the custodian or plan administrator is handling the transactions that are occurring in your account, you must be aware of what is going on and making sure that the transactions are appropriate. If funds are misplaced or not deposited timely into one of your employee's accounts, this could be an issue for you with the Department of Labor and could involve penalties and other fees. It is also good to keep in mind that you should be watching how the investments are performing. Again, while the custodian or plan administrator is in charge of your funds, you want to make sure that all funds chosen are performing as you would expect them.

You, and you alone, will be the one to make the deciding factor as to which investments should be offered.

# Chapter 5:
# Pros and Cons of a Self-Directed
# Retirement Plan

Let's look at some of the benefits and drawbacks of a self-directed plan in order to gain a better understanding of them. We will begin by discussing the benefits.

Previously, we mentioned that the earnings in a retirement account are not taxed until withdrawn. This gives us several tax advantages for owning real estate in a retirement account. Typically, the sale of real estate is a taxable event. You would calculate the gain from the sale and you would owe capital gains tax in the year sold. If the real estate sold is held in a retirement account, there is no capital gains tax. The funds remain in your account free to invest in other properties or however you see fit.

With no capital gains tax, more cash is available to make future investments. That extra cash could help you to reach the amount needed to make your next great investment a reality. For most people, this is by far the most popular benefit of purchasing real estate in a self-directed retirement plan.

Similar to buying real estate outright, there is no time limit for holding the investment property. For example, you can keep the real estate in your account for 1 year, 5 years, 20 years, or forever – in which case the property will be passed on to your beneficiary. It's completely your choice.

Another big benefit is the ability to leverage your retirement investment by obtaining financing from a bank. You can obtain financing from a bank or other institution to purchase real estate. However, the loan must be a non-recourse loan. This means that you cannot be personally liable to repay the loan in the case of a default. Typically, the only collateral for the loan will be the property itself. Your retirement funds will generally remain safe from the creditor as well. You may find this type of loan harder to acquire, but there are lenders out there who offer this as an option.

To illustrate the power of this benefit, let's look at an example. Suppose you have $100,000 in your retirement account. In a lot of markets, if you look for a good deal, this is enough to find and purchase a single family home and generate positive cash flow from renting. You purchase a $100,000 home and are able to generate monthly rents of $1,200. Since you don't have a mortgage, you get to keep the full amount to pay for repairs, taxes, etc. This equates to $14,400 for the year – pretty good.

If you instead find two properties worth $100,000, you can utilize a loan to purchase each one.

Perhaps the loan requires a 25% down payment, so you use $50,000 of your cash to get two $100,000 loans and purchase two rental properties. Each rental property generates $1,200 of monthly rents, but now you have to cover an estimated $400 monthly mortgage so you only net $800 per month per property. This equates to $9,600 for the year per property. Taking into account both properties, however, you are earning $19,200 a year – almost $5,000 more than buying a single property. Plus, you still have $50,000 of liquid cash in your retirement account for other investments.

The last benefit to mention is the ability to generate a larger rate of return on your investments. You are not limited by the often touted 10% average return for stocks. Or even less for bonds or money market funds. Of course, this depends on being able to find a good deal in the first place. But, your performance isn't tied to a market that fluctuates daily, nor is it held back by low rates of return on bonds or mutual funds. Keep in mind though, a larger rate of return is not guaranteed. Like any investment, there are risks involved.

Having real estate in a tax deferred retirement account also has some drawbacks. Depending on your real estate property, it's sometimes possible to have a positive cash flow while generating a tax loss. If the real estate is in a retirement plan, you are losing out on the potential tax benefit this can provide you on your personal tax return. That tax loss could be used to offset income you have from wages, self-employment activity, or other income. There are income limitations to this deduction, but for those who qualify this can be a sizable benefit that you are missing out on. With a truly great real estate deal, however, this drawback may not affect you at all.

It can be difficult to secure that great real estate deal. Mistakes happen. Let's say you invested in a real estate property and the value has gone down significantly. Now you wish to sell the property to get rid of it once and for all. You list it on the market and end up selling the property, incurring a large capital loss. Ordinarily, you would be able to offset other capital gains and then deduct an additional $3,000 against other income from the capital loss of selling an investment property. But, if the real estate property is in your retirement plan, you do not get the benefit of deducting the capital loss at all, including the additional deduction against other sources of income.

The final major drawback requires us to take a step back and look at the big picture of what we're doing. These are retirement accounts, the goal of which is to help supplement one's retirement income to maintain a certain lifestyle. Any investment is risky, but when dealing with retirement funds, sometimes that risk is simply not worth the chance of additional benefits. As the owner and decision maker of your self-directed retirement plan, you are ultimately responsible for any poor investment decisions made.

Your account could lose money – possibly lots of it. I hope this is not the case, but it cannot be ignored. It can be difficult to replenish your retirement funds and/or replace losses. You may not have the funds to replenish it, or the annual IRS contribution limits could be getting in your way. Be sure to keep this in mind when making all risk-related decisions related to your account.

# Chapter 6:
# Using the Self-Directed IRA LLC

Sometimes referred to as a "checkbook" IRA, a self-directed IRA LLC's goal is to eliminate the middle man, or the custodian, in order to streamline management of the IRA. As we will get to later, I generally do not recommend this structure.

The IRA LLC works by establishing a new entity and giving you control over that entity. First, a Limited Liability Company, or LLC, is formed and the IRA becomes the sole owner of this entity. Unlike other entity structures, an IRA is a permitted member for LLCs. And second, upon formation, you would name yourself manager of the LLC. Being the manager allows you to enter into business transactions on behalf of the LLC.

Many third party providers will help with the formation of the LLC. It is done at the state level, and the rules vary slightly from state to state. There are two primary documents that you will be using when you form the LLC. You will need the Articles of Organization (Articles) and the LLC Operating Agreement (Operating Agreement). Your Articles outline the requirements to start your LLC, and allow you to register your business with the state. Some states require that you have an Operating Agreement in place prior to registration. In others, this is not required, but it is highly recommended that you still draft a proper Operating Agreement. There are special provisions that can be added to the Operating Agreement, specifically alluding to using the LLC in an IRA LLC structure. Again, your third party provider will likely help you with the formation of the LLC and the preparation of these documents.

The LLC is a separate entity and should be treated as such. You will need to open a business bank account and track the accounting for the entity. In addition, many states have annual filing requirements and/or tax returns that are due. Fees for these filings range from nothing to $500 and beyond. The fees will depend on the state the LLC was formed in, and where it is doing business. That small annual fee could deplete thousands of dollars from your retirement account over time. This isn't something you can ignore. You will have to continuously monitor the LLC to make sure it remains in good standing with the state, which includes paying any fees and completing any annual filings.

Being the manager of the LLC puts you in control of the entity. You can make investments without having to wait for your custodian to approve them. You can write checks for the entity immediately – no need to pay your custodian fees to do this for you.

This time savings is huge, and could possibly let you invest in something that would otherwise be impossible.

The IRA LLC is self-directed by its nature. Since you do not have a custodian, there is nothing stopping the LLC from investing in real estate or other types of available investments. Of course, this also means there is no middle man to make sure you do not enter into a prohibited transaction or become involved with transactions with disqualified people. More discussion on these transactions and how to avoid them follow later in the book.

The LLC serves merely as a flow-through entity. All profits and losses flow directly to its members, which is the IRA in this case. As mentioned earlier, there are certain states that impose an annual report or tax return that must be paid to remain in good standing. Basically, anything that you could not do with an IRA directly, you also cannot do with the IRA LLC. You still have to worry about prohibited transactions. And you still have to worry about avoiding certain taxes (which we will also cover later). You may have to spend time and money consulting with others to make sure you are entering into proper transactions with the IRA LLC.

So, why do I not recommend the IRA LLC? To put it simply, the Solo 401(k) offers many of the same benefits combined with fewer risks and a better understanding of the rules surrounding it from the IRS. Though self-directed IRA LLCs have been around for several years, there is no clear guidance from the IRS about their use and the checkbook control that the manager gets. This is especially true in the typical 100% IRA ownership structure. Federal LLC rules indicate that a single member LLC is a disregarded entity for tax purposes – basically meaning it does not exist separately for tax purposes. Also, the IRS has not explicitly stated whether a checking account is exempt from IRA custody rules. The risk here is that the IRS could possibly deem all of the LLC's assets as having been distributed from the IRA and would subject them to taxation immediately. In summary, there is little authoritative guidance and the current rules are unclear surrounding the IRA LLC.

# Chapter 7:
# Solo 401(k) Plan vs. Self-Directed IRA LLC

**A**s mentioned in the previous chapter, I recommend the Solo 401(k) plan over the self-directed IRA LLC. The benefits are typically the same or better, and there is generally less paperwork and lower annual fees.

The Solo 401(k) plan is available to sole proprietors, independent contractors, self-employed individuals, partnerships, LLCs, S corporations, and C corporations. If you own, and are active in your business, you will likely be considered eligible so long as the business is truly a business that is trying to generate profits. This is true even if you work on your business on the side.

You cannot establish a Solo 401(k) plan if you have employees age 21 or older who work over 1,000 hours in a year. Your spouse does not count for this test. While there are no rules that state how much income the business must generate before setting up a Solo 401(k) plan, be aware that you should be making contributions to the plan on a consistent basis. You are trying to fund your retirement account after all. This same line of thinking also applies to the IRA LLC.

A Solo 401(k) plan is similar to an IRA LLC in that you have the ability to have checkbook control over the assets. A Solo 401(k) plan is considered a trust for tax purposes and must appoint a trustee. You can appoint yourself as the trustee. This will allow you to avoid going through a custodian to approve and execute investment decisions, much like you could with an IRA LLC.

A major benefit of the Solo 401(k) is that the contribution limits are higher than any other retirement plan. You can designate the contributions as Roth contributions if you wish. This would allow you to avoid taxation at the time you withdraw your balances. However, you will not be able to currently deduct these contributions.

You may be more comfortable contributing additional money because a Solo 401(k) plan offers a loan option. With the Solo 401(k), you can borrow up to $50,000 or half of your account value (whichever is less). You can use these funds for whatever you want. There is generally a small fee for taking out a loan. The only other catch is that you have to pay yourself interest when repaying the loan. The interest rate depends on the market rate at the time. But in reality, this may not be a bad thing. The interest paid helps replenish your account balance, and could be greater than the rate of your return of your plan in times of poor economic conditions. It also helps offset any potential losses due to not being able to compound your earnings in the account. A loan option is not available for IRA LLCs.

You can leverage the value of your Solo 401(k) plan without having to worry about the Unrelated Debt Financed Income (UDFI) tax. It's a little known tax, and a detailed discussion on the UDFI tax follows later in this book. This exception does not apply to IRA LLCs. There are other ways to avoid the UDFI tax for IRA LLCs, but this is not a concern at all for a Solo 401(k) plan. If you are planning to leverage your retirement account to secure loans and purchase additional investments, there is no better option than the Solo 401(k).

While the benefits are numerous, there are also a few downsides to the Solo 401(k) plan. Often, you will find that establishing the plan costs more than other types of plans. This higher initial fee does offset some of the annual filing burdens that you would face with an IRA LLC. However, coupled with the possibility of a higher recurring annual fee, the costs can add up quickly.

There is no annual reporting tax or other reporting requirement for a Solo 401(k) plan until you reach an account value of $250,000. If you are over this amount, you are required to file Form 5500 (or Form 5500-EZ) on an annual basis. Your 401(k) provider will typically help you with this – for a fee of course. The penalties for not filing this form are quite extensive.

As with the IRA LLC, compliance with all applicable rules rests with the trustee of the Solo 401(k) plan. If you are not sure whether a certain transaction or investment type is allowable in the plan, you must spend the time and resources to find the answer before you make any decisions. Help is available, but it almost always comes at a price.

# Chapter 8:
# People and Transactions to Avoid

**R**egardless of the type of retirement plan you wish to establish, there are transactions that you need to avoid. The risk of non-compliance surrounding any retirement plan is huge. If you engage in a prohibited transaction, the IRS can effectively nullify your IRA or other retirement account and deem the full value of your account as being distributed. This forces you to pay taxes on the distribution, along with any interest and penalties that may have accrued during that time. The tax burden can grow substantial rather quickly. Not to mention the fact that you will have just lost that money from your retirement account. You may find it difficult to replenish these funds, especially if the majority of the value came from a rollover.

There are three primary categories of transactions to avoid. The first category is the concept that neither you nor most people close to you can benefit from the transactions occurring in your retirement account. This is the underlying concept among all three categories. For example, if you own a rental property, you cannot rent the property to your son or daughter even if it's at market rates. Even though there is no financial benefit to your child, they are still enjoying the benefit of the property. The benefit does not have to be tangible – it can be implied or even be a future benefit. You have to look to the ultimate result of the transaction to determine its impact. For example, you can't circumvent the rule by renting your property to your unrelated friend, whom then sub-leases a room in the property to your child. Your child is still benefiting, and this is prohibited.

In the example above, your child is considered a disqualified person. Others include yourself, your spouse, your ancestors (parents, grandparents), other lineal descendents (children, grandchildren), and any spouse of a lineal descendant. Qualified people include your aunts and uncles, cousins, brothers and sisters, unrelated friends, and nieces and nephews.

The second category of prohibited transactions is the buying, selling, or exchanging of property between your retirement plan and a disqualified person (including yourself). For example, let's say you recently bought a new home and you want to convert your old residence into a rental. Under normal tax circumstances, that's completely fine. But for a retirement account, that's a problem. You have no way of legally transferring the title to your retirement account even when using your retirement plan's funds to purchase the property. Since you are effectively contributing the old property to your own retirement account, this is not allowed. Again, even if you sold the property to yourself at market prices – this would be a prohibited transaction.

This category also covers the lending of funds from your account. Providing loans is an allowable investment for a self-directed retirement account, but you cannot provide loans to disqualified people. If your unrelated friend (a qualified person) is trying to get his business off the ground, you are allowed to loan them money and earn interest on that note. There is only a problem if you lend money to a disqualified person. Again, you must look at the end result of where the money went. You cannot lend money to a friend's business if you also have a 10% stake in the company. Since you are benefiting, even passively, this would be considered a prohibited transaction.

The third category of prohibited transactions is the inability for disqualified people to provide goods, services, or the use of facilities to the retirement plan. If you own a rental property, you cannot personally make repairs or perform maintenance on the property. For example, you cannot fix an appliance, change a light bulb, or even mow the lawn. You can hire someone to do this for you, provided that individual is not a disqualified person. You cannot furnish the property with your personal belongings. You cannot store items, machinery, or appliances for a rental property in your personal tool shed. Almost everything between you (or other disqualified people) must remain separate from your rental property. We will discuss in the next chapter what things you can do. The list is quite small.

# Chapter 9:
## So What Can I Do?

The IRS does not want you building sweat equity in your property. There are far more things you cannot do with your property than things you can do. This chapter will explain the items that you can do with your property. If an item is not listed here, chances are it is a prohibited transaction and you should assume you should not do it unless you already know otherwise. If you have any doubt whether an action would be prohibited or not, you should check with a professional before you do it. Don't wait until after the fact to see if it is okay. The items listed here apply to your property regardless of which type of retirement account it is being held in.

Probably the most important thing you can do is select and purchase the property you desire. This book does not cover the aspect of finding a great deal, but there are several resources available. Whether you are new to real estate investing, or a seasoned veteran, you can always learn something from others in this area. Don't fall into the trap of investing in a property solely for any perceived tax benefit. If it's a bad deal, it's a bad deal. The tax benefits will not change that.

Soon after purchasing a rental property, you'll likely have to complete some repairs prior to making it available for rent. You cannot do any of the repairs yourself, no matter how small. What you can do is choose who to hire to perform the work. You can request bids and inspect the work to make sure it's done properly. You have the authority to hire and fire as many contractors as you need. This same rule continues to apply after the property becomes occupied. It applies to almost everything you can think of – including repairs, maintenance, inspections, appliance replacements, etc.

Let's assume that you have made the initial repairs and now you start getting some rental applications for people who are interested in the property. You can, in fact, screen the tenants. You can meet with them, tour the property together, perform any necessary background checks, and discuss the terms of the agreement. You can have direct control over this aspect if you desire. If you have a multi-tenant property, you can evaluate all vacancies and fill them as needed.

After you have a tenant comes the best part – getting paid. You can collect the security deposit and rental fees. You can physically go to the property and collect the money, if you wish. When the time comes, you can evaluate current rental rates and decide to decrease or increase them, if needed.

In certain rare cases, you may have to evict the tenant. It is possible to do this on your own, but I don't recommend it. Should this situation arise, I recommend speaking with a professional familiar with the process and letting them handle the eviction.

The last item that I will mention is that you have control over the sale of the property. You can decide when, if ever, you wish to sell the property and how you want to market it. Remember, you cannot sell the property to, or for, the benefit of any disqualified people – as discussed in the previous chapter.

# Chapter 10:
# Taxes on Self-Directed Plans and How to Avoid Them

**D**epending on how you decide to hold and purchase your real estate, taxes could become a factor. There are two taxes to be aware of: the Unrelated Debt Financed Income (UDFI) tax and the Unrelated Business Income Tax (UBIT).

The UDFI tax applies when you are leveraging your retirement account and borrowing funds to purchase investment properties. If you use borrowed funds to acquire the property, you will be subject to this tax if your rental property is operating at a profit. The tax rate is 35% and is applied on a pro rata basis. For example, if you purchased a property for $100,000 and $70,000 of that came from a loan, then 70% of your profits from that property will be subject to this tax. So, if your rental income minus all your expenses came to $1,430, you would owe approximately $350 in taxes for the year ($1,430 * 70% * 35%). This is obviously a simplified look at this tax. The calculations can get complex rather quickly.

There are two primary methods for minimizing this tax. The first method is utilizing the depreciation deduction to reduce or zero out any profit from the property. Simply stated, the annual depreciation deduction for a property is the building's basis (not including land) divided by 27.5 years for a residential property or 39 years for a commercial property. With the depreciation deduction, it's possible to have positive cash flow from the property while showing a book loss.

For example: let's say you collected $12,000 in rent for a single family home for the year, and you had operating expenses of $9,000 (not including depreciation). The $9,000 is made up of repairs, maintenance, real estate taxes, and mortgage interest. Without depreciation, you would show a profit of $3,000 on the property – which is pretty good. If we assume the basis of the building is $110,000, then the depreciation deduction would be equal to $4,000 (or $110,000 / 27.5). This would mean your actual book loss is $1,000 (or $3,000 profit less the $4,000 of depreciation). And because of that, you would not owe any UDFI tax.

The second method was mentioned earlier in this book – if you choose to use a Solo 401(k) plan to purchase and hold your real estate investments, the UDFI tax will not apply to you. The tax is not levied on Solo 401(k) plans.

The UBIT applies to the income of an unrelated trade or business regularly carried on. In the case of a self-directed plan, pretty much any business activity will be treated as unrelated to its exempt purpose. There is no strict definition of a business being regularly carried on. It depends on the activity, and the facts and circumstances of the situation.

In the context of real estate investments, the UBIT applies to house flipping activity. The problem is that there is no clear line for what level of flipping is needed to trigger the tax. If you purchase a home, put some work into it over time, and it goes up in value after a couple years and you want to sell it, that's okay. Having just that one home sale in a two year period will not trigger the UBIT. Having one to two sales in a one year period is probably okay. But, any more than that and you risk triggering the UBIT. With tax rates going up to 39.6%, this is certainly something you want to avoid. If house flipping is your goal, then a self-directed retirement account may not be the right choice for you.

# Chapter 11:
# How to Fund Your Self-Directed Plan

$\mathbf{A}$t this point in the book, we've made it through the bulk of the technical detail behind self-directed retirement plans. The next few chapters will outline how to get your plan up and running, and some of the things that you should expect to see with your new plan. In this chapter, we will talk about funding your plan.

There are two primary methods for funding your retirement account. These methods are the same regardless of which type of plan you choose to set-up. The two methods are: making annual contributions and rolling over funds from another retirement plan.

Annual contributions are subject to certain limits depending on the plan you have and the amount of income you make from your business. If you can afford to do so, you should make these contributions every year. Most plans allow for an electronic transfer from your bank account, or you can usually write a check if you prefer. You can choose to make the contribution all at once, or divide it out over the year – it's completely up to you. Your advisor will help you determine how much you can contribute and by what point in time the funds must be received in order to be attributed to the correct year.

Rolling over funds from another retirement account is a flexible option that can add substantially more funds to your plan than making annual contributions. Generally, there is no limit to the amount of funds that you can roll into a plan. Rolling over funds is the fastest and easiest way to get started with a self-directed plan. However, it is only available to those who currently have a funded retirement account.

There are two types of rollovers available: direct and indirect rollovers. With a direct rollover, when structured properly, the funds transfer between your retirement accounts and there are no penalties or taxes involved. An indirect rollover, on the other hand, occurs when the distribution is issued to the plan participant, and the participant in turn then contributes the funds to another retirement plan. Taxes are required to be withheld for this type of transaction, and there are strict time limits for when the funds must be contributed to the new plan. It is almost always easier and more beneficial to do a direct rollover.

There is some flexibility in terms of which accounts can be rolled into your new self-directed plan. Let's take a look at one of the more common examples among traditional/pre-tax retirement plans. Let's say you have been contributing annually to either a traditional IRA account or your employer's sponsored plan (such as a 401(k) plan), if they offer one. You now decide you want to start your own business, and with that, you open a new self-directed retirement plan. Regardless of whether you choose a self-directed IRA (including the IRA LLC structure) or a Solo 401(k) plan, you are eligible to rollover your funds from your old account into your new one. For example, you can move your 401(k) funds to your new self-directed IRA. Or you can move your traditional IRA account into a new Solo 401(k) plan.

Your advisor will inform you of the process of directly rolling over funds, but it can be broken down into the following four steps:

1. Open your new self-directed account
2. Find out the information needed to rollover funds to the new account – for example, to whom should the check be made out
3. Contact your old retirement account holder and give them permission and the instructions for distributing the funds from your account
4. Your new self-directed account will receive the funds and deposit them into your plan

Come January or February, you will receive IRS Form 1099-R. This form informs both you and the

IRS of the details of the transaction. You must report the transaction on your tax return, but since it will be coded as a rollover, it is generally not considered taxable.

# Chapter 12:
# Questions to Ask

**A**s you start to research the various plans available, you will find that no two are alike. The services offered by the plan administrator will vary. Prices are different. Some plans may even limit certain types of investments. As mentioned earlier in the book, ultimately it is your plan and your responsibility.

The following list of questions is not all-inclusive, but it should give you a head start in the right direction for choosing a plan that is best suited for you:

- Do you offer a free initial consultation?
- Are there limits to the types of investments I can make?
- Who is responsible for filing the required tax returns? Do you offer support to help with these? If so, how much does this cost?
- What is your pricing structure? If an annual fee, are there any other potential

charges during the year? For example: a charge for excess transactions.

- For an IRA LLC, will you help with the formation and ongoing requirements? Is there an added cost for this?
- What is your rollover process? What types of plans can I rollover funds from?
- How can I contribute funds to the plan? For example: write a check or electronic debit.
- Will I have a dedicated account representative?
- How quickly do you process transactions?
- Is there a minimum balance for my account?
- Are there any set-up fees?
- Are you available for assistance with IRS issues?

Sometimes the best resources are current customers. Look for testimonials and/or reviews about the company. Ask around, maybe you will find someone you know that has a self-directed plan. Talk to them about how they like their provider, if they would recommend them, or things to look out for in general.

# Chapter 13:
# Process of Using a Plan to Purchase Real Estate

**R**egardless of which provider you choose to use, the overall process for purchasing real estate in a self-directed retirement plan will be pretty similar. Following is a general 10-step outline for purchasing real estate in a self-directed retirement plan:

1. Find, open, and fund a self-directed retirement plan of your choosing.
2. Locate a property to purchase. Remember, just because you are buying the property in a tax advantageous fashion does not mean you should not be selective. Do your research, take your time and try to find a great deal.
3. Once you find a property, keep in mind it is your retirement plan that is buying the property – not you.
4. Work with your provider and have them sign an offer to purchase the property.

5. Many deals require a deposit (typically called an earnest money deposit) from the buyer. If this is the case, you must submit a letter (or some form of instruction) to your provider for the earnest money deposit with the dollar amount needed along with supporting documentation.

6. If all goes well, and you end up purchasing the property, now you have to pay for it. Typically, funds will be wired directly from your retirement plan to the seller.

7. Now the purchase has been funded and the sale can be recorded. Congratulations!

8. Hire contractors to fix up the property if needed. Pay them directly from your retirement plan.

9. Find and screen for a good tenant. Your tenant must pay their rent to your retirement plan directly. Refer to Chapter 8 to make sure you do not benefit a disqualified person.

10. Use contractors to maintain the property. Keep good records. Reap the benefits of your new investment.

# Chapter 14:
# Next Steps

**W**here you go from here is up to you. Maybe you started off thinking you wanted a self-directed IRA, but now you feel like a Solo 401(k) plan would work best. Maybe you decided that the extra work for maintaining rental real estate in a self-directed plan is not worth the hassle. Or perhaps you just wanted to learn more about self-directed plans. Whatever it is, my hope is that the information presented here can help you make a more informed decision.

If you do decide to move forward, the very first thing you need to do is find a provider who is willing to work with you and help you through the process. Look to Chapter 12 for some guidance – there is no one-size-fits-all solution for everyone. As such, I cannot recommend one provider over any others. Do your research, listen to your gut, and make it happen!

40147820R00033

Made in the USA
San Bernardino, CA
24 June 2019